LYRICAL

LYRICAL

Poems That Could Become Songs

ℬ

ALLAN HUGH COLE JR.
MEREDITH C. COLE

RESOURCE *Publications* · Eugene, Oregon

LYRICAL
Poems That Could Become Songs

Resource Publications
An Imprint of Wipf and Stock Publishers
199 W. 8th Ave., Suite 3
Eugene, OR 97401

www.wipfandstock.com

PAPERBACK ISBN: 979-8-3852-4228-3
HARDCOVER ISBN: 979-8-3852-4229-0
EBOOK ISBN: 979-8-3852-4230-6

For Travis Foster, talented teacher and faithful friend

To a father growing old, nothing is dearer than a daughter.
    —Euripides

Without music, life would be a mistake.
    —Friedrich Nietzsche

Contents

CONTENTS

Acknowledgments

ONE OF US (MEREDITH) has been a singer and musician for nearly as long as she's been in the world. The other one of us (Allan) started playing music at the age of fifty-five, after Meredith (his daughter) challenged him to pursue a lifelong interest in learning to play a musical instrument—namely, bass guitar. He answered her challenge, and it transformed his life.

As a father and daughter, we play and write music together. You may think of this book as a collection of lyrics we have written that could become songs. We also play music regularly with our band, the JAMBS, which includes our valued friends: Jason Meeker, Joel Knutson, Baker Hamilton, and Shawn Lein. All of us met as students at the Austin School of Rock, which has been, for both of us, way station, dream catcher, sanctuary, and extended family. Playing with the JAMBS is similarly special and life giving for us.

We express our profound gratitude to many folks at the Austin School of Rock: Dustie Shelton, general manager; Travis Foster, music director; Ian MacDougal, assistant music director; Amanda Wisniewski, studio coordinator; and a group of talented teachers and generous humans who touch, shape, and transform the lives of people ages six and up through the power of music taught and played: Jason McMaster, Sage Glasscock, Ahmed Garcia, Zeke Zimmerman, Hannah Devereaux, Jamey Simms, Nick Hughes, and many more. Individually and collectively, they have helped us heal, grow, and improve in many aspects of our lives, music included.

We also want to thank our publishing team, led so ably by Matthew Wimer. A wise and thoughtful human, not only does he serve with distinction as managing editor at Wipf and Stock, but he is also an accomplished musician and teacher of music. We deeply appreciate his support for this project as well as his guidance, which always contributes to higher quality work. The entire team at Wipf and Stock, which continues to set a high bar in publishing, also made significant contributions to this project. We are grateful to have worked with such stellar colleagues and people.

One School of Rock superhuman, Travis Foster, who has served as music teacher for both of us, deserves special mention and words of thanks. We know of no one who has helped more people through music to find their voice, tap their talents, quash their self-doubt, or reclaim their lives—whether from teenage angst or Parkinson's disease—than Travis has. His grace, graciousness, generosity, and talent are extraordinary gifts to those who know him. Musically and in terms of friendship, he is exemplary!

As much as anything else, Travis embodies the timeless truth that to be kind is to be most human.

We dedicate this book to Travis.

Allan Cole and Meredith Cole
Austin, Texas
September 30, 2025

Before Goodbye

Allan Cole

Thunder looms nearby
I look up and taste the rain
Clouds cover blue skies
Tell me why. Oh, tell me why

Living slowly helps us see
Acting boldly helps us believe
Life makes us laugh, makes us cry
Tell me why. Please, tell me why

Love endures, deceit obscures
Honest people do what they should
Kindness never gets old
Forgiving repairs the soul

If only we could.
If only we could

To err is human, to forgive, divine
Seeking truth, top of mind
Healing within means trusting again
Tell me why before goodbye
Before goodbye, tell me why

Kind ones give, we can too
Pull from yourself, live more true

Point to what's sacred for you
Before goodbye, tell me why
Tell me why before goodbye

Love endures, deceit obscures
Honest people do what they should
Kindness never gets old
Forgiving repairs the soul

If only we could.
If only we could.

Taste the rain, it helps the pain
Forgive yourself, others too
Taste the rain, and tell me why
Before goodbye, tell me why

Tell me why, before goodbye

The Songs I Used to Know

Meredith Cole

The Rosedale house was purple
And passion-vine flowers grew
Sometimes we still drive by it
That special place I knew

Then the world seemed bigger
Or was it that I was smaller?
The house, she looks so different
Now that I am taller

I think back to those days and start to grieve
When did I stop making believe?

Mom asked me what I was humming
I heard it long ago
If I close my eyes, I can almost remember
The songs I used to know

Our shed was my house
When I used to pretend
When did I start to see
A shed as just a shed?

I remember when Dad would take us
To the park to play
I rode my bike with courage
And my training wheels went away

I think back to those days and start to grieve
When did I stop making believe?

Mom asked me what I was humming
I heard it long ago
If I close my eyes, I can almost remember
The songs I used to know

The Rosedale house still stands, as the years quickly fly by
It will either be torn down or wither away with time
Just like me, it ages, the purple paint chipping
The memories, once vivid, have recently been slipping

The songs I once sang vanish, their melodies die

Goodbye

Wise Ones Know

Allan Cole

Wise ones know you can lose
What you have, what has you
Know you keep what is true
Who you love, who loves you

If we seek, we can find
What matters most outlasts time
Sages get it, Holy Ones too
What about me and you?

Wise ones know it's love we need
Love given, love received
Risking love sets us free
Lets you be you and me be me

Searched for years and didn't know
Living real helps me grow
Be more myself, give more of me
Give more to life, live more free

Finding meaning offers beauty
Expecting joy is our duty
Tomorrow's pain is for another day
Loving madly provides a way

Wise ones know it's love we need
Love given, love received
Risking love sets us free
Lets you be you and me be me

Risking love eases pain
Filling hearts is love's refrain
Eyes can see what stays true
Hearts see it too, for me and you

A younger me had it wrong
Life is short, never long
Let's not waste a moment more
Love madly, and love some more

Wise ones know it's love we need
Love given, love received
Risking love sets us free
Lets you be you and me be me

Pages

Meredith Cole

Just one more page, can't put this book down
until the heroes prevail
Used to do the same, now I know, the devil's in the details

Have you ever hung on a cliffhanger?
Painted landscapes in your mind?
Taken the long way home, just for a laugh?
And stopped waiting for the stars to align?

Not knowing can get you goin'
Like a river that keeps on flowin'
Worrying less gives you more
Time for dreamin' 'bout what's in store

Life feels formulaic
'Cause plots never thicken
Tappin' my foot as I wait, if only time would quicken

Have you ever made a wish
While not knowing what you'd wish for?
Run before you walked, wearing mismatched socks
Or played games without keeping score?

Not knowing can get you goin'
Like a river that keeps on flowin'
Worrying less gives you more

Time for dreamin' 'bout what's in store

The beauty's in the read, you can be at peace
When we enjoy each chapter, our stories are complete
Yeah, the beauty's in the read

Questions

Allan Cole

Dogs gnaw on rawhide bones
Wind blows cold, leaves me alone
Where do I go? When do I see?
Should I stay or should I leave?

Questions come easy, always have
Schools and degrees, a go-to salve
Time will make parchment fade
Do I go or do I stay?

I think when I play, see when I sing
Wake early each day, relearn who I am
What I should do, what I can say
Who believes in me every day?

Why am I here?
For others, for them
My big three
All brilliant, lovely gems

Lives fitting together
Like hands-in-gloves
Investing in love
Unwavering love

I think when I play, see when I sing

Wake early each day, relearn who I am
What I should do, what I can say
Who believes in me every day?

We laugh and cry
Say hello and goodbye
Speak the truth
With no need for words

We dream and share
Wander and roam
Sing our songs
While dogs gnaw bones

I think when I play, see when I sing
Wake early each day, relearn who I am
What I should do, what I can say
Who believes in me every day?

Dandelion Days

Meredith Cole

We embark on an evening stroll
I skip and walk on my tiptoes
Fireflies dance in the darkening skies
As the day and the sunshine say their goodbyes

I pick a dandelion
And hold it in the palm of my hand
I blow, and those delicate seeds dance
Floating away in the wind

I wonder where each seed will land
When the wind stops blowing
Will they make it to earthy ground?
And begin again, safe and sound?

I pick a dandelion
And hold it in the palm of my hand
I blow, and those delicate seeds dance
Floating away in the wind

Little fairies of floating fluff
Gracefully gliding with ease
They go wherever the wind may blow
Guided by the breeze

I can't stop time, though you know I try
I'll hold your hand and never let go
But the sun always sets, the embers die
I try to believe, but you never know

You are a dandelion
I hold you in the palm of my hand
I hope that someday you won't leave me
Floating away in the wind

The Teacher

Allan Cole

He helps you learn your way
Loses track of the mistakes
Sings loud when feeling low
Talented and raring to go

He can riff with the best
All day long, with no rest
Sees the world in more vivid ways
Finds meaning every day

Learning means discerning
Testing means reflecting
Diplomas fade with time
Pain lights the mind

He loves playing, that's for sure
Loves teaching even more
Challenges you to explore
To trust yourself and feel secure

I met him when I needed to
A special human living true
Face outlined by a bucket hat
He helped me re-find my path

Learning means discerning
Testing means reflecting
Diplomas fade with time
Pain lights the mind

A teacher, a cherished friend
Together we discern and look within
Trying to live what stays true
We sing and play, and our souls renew

You have teachers too
Those who walk with you
Whether young or old
They listen and help heal your soul

Learning means discerning
Testing means reflecting
Diplomas fade with time
Teachers light the mind

Decisions, Decisions

Meredith Cole

I played dress up as a kid
A chef or an attorney
For the day, I'd play, then take off my costume
Who do I really want to be?

I'm decisively indecisive
Toward what I want and need
Am I on the right path?
I just hope to succeed

Dad, I'm scared
I'm scared of the future
The uncertainty it will bring

Mom, I worry I'll waste my potential
Don't let me spend my life lazing

I beg you, Holly, be honest with me
Point out the flaws I'm too blind to see

Just me and my thoughts, head tangled in knots
Decisions, decisions, decisions, and me

Dad, I'm really freaking out
Please call when you have a chance
I feel like a failure, a major loser
Like I'm stuck in a rut and will never advance

When did I become complacent?
Falling behind the rest
What should I do? How do I push through?
And fix the problems within myself?

Dad, I'm scared
I'm scared of the future,
The uncertainty it will bring

Mom, I worry I'll waste my potential
Please don't let me spend my life lazing

I beg you, Holly, be honest with me
Point out the flaws I'm too blind to see

Just me and my thoughts, head tangled in knots
Decisions, decisions, decisions, and me

I gained weight and lost motivation
A shell of who I used to be
Have I gotten dumber? That'd be a bummer
Or is that another irrational worry?

I worry about school, I worry about life
Overthinking all I do and say
Viewing my life, in black and white
Help me to see the shades of grey

We all doubt ourselves, it's true
Especially the greats, like Mom and you
How do I face my fears and decide?
Decisions make me want to hide

Dad, I'm scared
I'm scared of the future,
The uncertainty it will bring

Mom, I worry I'll waste my potential
Please don't let me spend my life lazing

I beg you, Holly, be honest with me
Point out the flaws I'm too blind to see

Just me and my thoughts, head tangled in knots
Decisions, decisions, decis—

Burned

Allan Cole

It's true
I believed in you
Told others they should to
Before you burned me, through and through

Despite suspicion and intuition
I kept investing in you
Believed your words rang true
Defended your reputation too

I remained a friend
Trustworthy to the end
Stayed loyal
Like I always do

Never questioned your character
Nor thought you'd turn
Couldn't imagine a world
Where . . . by you I'd be burned

Another trustworthy one
Came my way
Your empty promises
Convinced me to stay

I remained a friend
Trustworthy to the end
Stayed loyal
Like I always do

Reiterating your plan
Repeating big dreams
You and me and another
The so-called faithful three

I bet on you
Trusted your word
Held it sacred and strong
Sang the friendship song

I remained a friend
Trustworthy to the end
Stayed loyal
Like I always do

Believing in you carried me on—
You assured me I belonged
Urged me to trust you
Which I did

I was wrong.

Plato's Cave

Meredith Cole

How can you describe the sun
If you've only seen the cave?
Shadows bouncing on the walls
Never seen the light of day

Break your chains and step outside
See the world with your own eyes
They won't believe the things you say
If they only know the cave

Color means nothing if you've never seen
Pain means nothing if you never bleed
What you do and where you go
Dictates everything you know

Sound means nothing if you've never heard
Language means nothing if you can't read words
To see the world you need to be brave
Maybe we're all prisoners in Plato's cave

If you've only seen the darkness
How do you know that you aren't blind?
Living life with your back to the fire
What's there to lose when it's time to die?

I have loved and I have lost
I've had to learn and I've had to grow
There's so little that I've seen
There's so little that I know

Color means nothing if you've never seen
Pain means nothing if you never bleed
What you do and where you go
Dictates everything you know

Sound means nothing if you've never heard
Language means nothing if you can't read words
To see the world you need to be brave
Maybe we're all prisoners in Plato's cave

What is the meaning of life?
Why are we here?
Where do we go after we die?
Am I in Plato's cave?

So, if you think you know the world
Is that true or are you blind?
Do you know the games life plays
Or are you also in the cave?

One Plus One

Allan Cole

No need for alarms
Sleep is hardly a thought
Time is short
Can never be bought

Using the day
Keeps it from using me
Singing new songs
Where I need to be

Time marches on
It always will
What happens in time
Can harm or heal
Memories build
If we allow them to
One plus one
Can be more than two

A new day's sun
Can shine on joy
Let us love
More than before

Teach us that less
Can be more
Show us that less
Can be more

Time marches on
It always will
What happens in time
Can harm or heal
Memories build
If we allow them to
One plus one
Can be more than two

Now we know
What's at stake each day
Each moment
As we make our way

The path has curves
Roadblocks too
Hearts get ripped from
Our bodies—true

Time marches on
It always will
What happens in time
Can harm or heal
Memories build
If we allow them to
One plus one
Can be more than two

When love remains
We find a balm
It soothes the pain
Carries us on

Our friends heal us
With laughter and tears
Give life meaning
Help us live again

When harder days come
I will lean on you
Lean on me too
As friends do

Time marches on
It always will
What happens in time
Can harm or heal
Memories build
If we allow them to
One plus one
Can be more than two

Life renews
When meeting one
Who touches us
Deep within

We cannot outlast time
But we can live, grow, and dream
We cannot outlast time
But we can sing.

30 Hours a Day

Meredith Cole

Walked down the stairs to hell
Never thought I'd sell
My soul to the man below

Thought I could do it all
I'd rather die than fall
To the temptation of the dark

"Would you like some money?" he said
"Or perhaps you'd like true love instead?"
"Thank you, but I'm fine.
I only want more time."

I only get one life
For myself, my job, my wife
My kids and parents, my hobbies too
Too little time, too much to do

"Would you like some money?" he said
"Or perhaps you'd like true love instead?"
"Thank you, but I'm fine.
I only want more time."

Feet scorched on the molten floor
The burning in my soul hurt more
What would a good man pay?
For 30 hours a day?

"Would you like some money?" he said
"Or perhaps you'd like true love instead?"
"Thank you, but I'm fine.
I only want more time."

Time is money, money's time, seconds are pennies, minutes are dimes

Places to Stay

Allan Cole

A change of plans made my day
Gave me time in places to stay
Grabbed my bass wearing a grin
Making music with friends

Life has takers acting swole
Also givers wrapping souls
Givers stand ready to play
Let me sing and let me sway

Life makes sense, life is strange
Givers and takers, joy and pain
Living teaches losers can gain
If we find places to stay

She was first to show the way
Speaking promises we both made
Standing tall, she said, *You'll be OK*
Our promises mean we'll be OK

Daughters make life complete
Fill my heart and dreams in sleep
One gives music, one gives play
Love grows in places to stay

Life makes sense, life is strange
Givers and takers, joy and pain
Living teaches losers can gain
If we find places to stay

Love means takers cannot win
Love is music that never ends
Be a giver, do what you say
Promise to love, come what may

Others make me a better man
Husband and father, son and friend
Generous faces, compassionate grins
Fill my places again and again

Life makes sense, life is strange
Givers and takers, joy and pain
Living teaches losers can gain
If we find places to stay
If we find places to stay

Dad

Meredith Cole

You see the patch of sunshine
Shining through a wall of grey
Basking in its warmth
While the rain around us pours

Accepting those around you
Choosing kindness indefinitely
Picking the apple with a bruise
That nobody else would choose

You are so special
In all you say and do
You are my hero
Everyone should be a bit more like you

How are you so patient?
You deal with more than most
Facing illness, a smile on your face
As we sing a song while you play bass

You give those around you everything
Keeping promises when I break mine
There the minute I say I'm in need
You always make time for your family

You are so special
In all you say and do
You are my hero
The world could stand to learn a lot from you

You're no longer a preacher
But you practice what you preach
The greatest kind of teacher
The one that loves to teach

My words hurt you in anger
I've taken you for granted
And yet you see the best in me
When I don't deserve it

My dad is so special
Everyone knows it's true
So thank you, Dad, for loving me
I really, really love you too

Fast as Friends

Allan Cole

He sees her smile
She sees him grin
With muscle cars and Lone Stars
They're fast as friends

Dancing around feelings
Throwing caution to the wind
Close to the starting line
Feeling alive again

He dreams of her
each night and day
Wonders if she'll ever
think of him that way

She's thought it a thousand times
They could go all in
With muscle cars and Lone Stars
They're fast as friends

With muscle cars and Lone Stars
They're fast as friends

Hitting a hundred
About to break a sweat
Both being gamblers
Would they make the bet?

Started feeling risky
Too much to lose
When a heart starts drifting
Other hearts can bruise

Throttling motors and
Pumping brakes
No line gets crossed
No hearts will ache

Still, motors run forever
with some fuel and a little care
If only in their dreams
They can still get there

When tomorrow comes
Will they dance again?
Will their moments feel
Like losses or wins?

He saw her smile
She saw him grin

With muscle cars and Lone Stars
They were fast as friends

With muscle cars and Lone Stars
They were fast as friends

Strength

Meredith Cole

She ran a marathon
When she planned to do half
She never complains
Just fights through the pain

Rises at the crack of dawn
But still gets right to work
Spends the hours baking
Labors without breaking

In her kindness there is strength
She's a warrior of compassion
Caring for every living thing
As four dogs bark and baby birds sing

She's not afraid to speak her mind
'Bout the state of the world
Always in the know
Always on the go

She helps me when I'm feeling down
But tells me to keep going
Comforting me with a hug
She's as tough as her tough love

In her kindness there is strength
She's a warrior of compassion
Caring for every living thing
As four dogs bark and baby birds sing

A storm wrecked the flowers
That you worked so hard to tend
But just like you they persevered
And began to grow again

In her kindness there is strength
She's a warrior of compassion
Caring for every living thing
As four dogs bark and baby birds sing

One Chance, One Moment

Allan Cole

One chance, one moment
A gentleman says
Eyes shining kindness
A bow of his head

Four words reveal
A frame of mind
One chance, one moment
A life we can find

We need compassion and simplicity
Won't you bow your head with me
One chance, one moment can make us free
We need compassion and simplicity

Anger fills the world today
How exactly did we lose our way?
Love is where we begin anew
We can live this sacred truth

Kindness starts with trust
We know abides
Compassion means we suffer
When another cries

Held together
By simplicity
One chance, one moment
We can learn all three

We need compassion and simplicity
Won't you bow your head with me
One chance, one moment
Can make us free
We need compassion and simplicity

It began in Japan
With a gentle man
He spoke to me
I could see

One chance, one moment
You and me
Peace, love, compassion
Simplicity

Thank You

Meredith Cole

I was starving one night, and you fed me
Then you taught me to fish, feeding me for a lifetime
When there was drought, you were the rain
I needed rescuing, you sent a lifeline

You led me through the forest
Taught me the way back home
I don't need to be saved anymore
I can do it on my own

You tipped the scale by showing me
I'm worth my weight in gold
Your tough love has made me tougher, it's true
So thank you

You're Prometheus, you gave me my fire
Ignited a spark when I needed it
Embers were fading, I tended the flames
Kindled them wisely, they haven't depleted yet

I used to feel so little
A sailboat lost at sea
You saw my smoke signal
Others were deaf, but you could still hear me

You tipped the scale by showing me
I'm worth my weight in gold
Your tough love has made me tougher, it's true
So thank you

Stranded in a desert of doubt
You were an oasis
The calm before and during the storm
The embodiment of homeostasis

You tipped the scale by showing me
I'm worth my weight in gold
Your tough love has made me tougher, it's true
So thank you

Dream Catcher

Allan Cole

She caught my eye
Stepping inside
I hit the floor
Wanting more
Wanting more

You can't stop hearts
Once they soar
My, oh my
Souls starting to roar

I met a dream catcher, what can she do?
I met a dream catcher, what can she do?

What can I say?
What feels true?
Since we met
I haven't been blue

She likes to think
When we drink
I think my brain is growing
Will it ever shrink?

I met a dream catcher, what can we do?
I met a dream catcher, what can we do?

She caught my eye
There with another guy
Feelings mostly inside
Now and then I cry

Left with her big lie
Fear a timeless guide
Still, I want to try
My dreams feel alive

I met a dream catcher, what can I do?
I met a dream catcher, what can I do?
I met a dream catcher, what can I do?
I met a dream catcher, what can I do?

Not a Friend of Mine

Meredith Cole

She doesn't listen to me
Goes deaf when I tell her no
Holds me back from trying new things
Says "you'll die if you go"

God-like endurance, can't outrun her
A Riptide personified, pulling me under

She's not a friend of mine
But still, she sticks around
Someone I run into
When my guard is down

I can't get rid of her
I bet you know her too
Showing up to parties she wasn't invited to

She's the queen of diatribes
I have no choice but to listen
A self-righteous artist
Won't let me question her vision

She's an assassin, killed me a thousand times
A con woman, never tried for her crimes

She's not a friend of mine
But still, she sticks around
Someone I run into
When my guard is down

I can't get rid of her
I bet you know her too
Showing up to parties she wasn't invited to

Stealing my energy
Feeding me lies
Her antics come in an endless supply
I can't get rid of her, not a chance
All I can do is build tolerance

She's not a friend of mine
But still, she sticks around
Someone I run into
When my guard is down

I can't get rid of her
I bet you know her too
Showing up to parties she wasn't invited to

Heart Songs

Allan Cole

You sing, I change
Heart fills, soul renews
Greatest joys long revealed
Deepest hopes becoming real

Saw the hard times you faced
So unfair and lacking grace
Wanted to shield you in every way
From pain hard to erase

A new dream comes true today
On a stage where we play
Heart overflowing for all to see
Your melodies giving life to me

Your challenge, made so sly
Your example, the reason why
I made excuses, you stayed cool
Your love carrying me back to school

This is the day
Beside you on stage
Warm lights outline your face
Pride and joy rolling through me

Playing heart songs that heal me
Fueled by love you give me
Today, pain moves away
I'm beside you on the stage

A new dream comes true today
On a stage where we play
Heart overflowing for all to see
Your melodies giving life to me

On Behalf of My Insecurity

Meredith Cole

The table doesn't need to know
I have aces in my hand
Winners keep it on the down-low
Humility trumps arrogance

But among my aces, I have the old maid
My insecurity
So I feel the need to compensate
By sharing my victories

I'm not who you think I am
And that's not a fact I hide
I'm in solitary confinement with my self-doubt
As I sit in my room and cry

Don't want to be a bragger
Or make anyone feel less than
Can't lose to my anxiety
I can't become a villan

I know the feeling
How badly it can hurt
When someone fuels their ego
By attacking yours

I'm not who you think I am
I just want to hide
On behalf of my insecurity
I apologize

Brown Eyes

Allan Cole

Patience, love, integrity
The more given, the more received
On hard days that worry me
Brown eyes under blue skies

Sowing joy, waging peace
Hoping illness will someday cease
Birds singing, dogs dreaming
Brown eyes capture me

I see brown eyes under blue skies
Enjoy sunny days, time to play
A life that's sweet, not pain free
Brown eyes fill my need.

Glasses help me see the page
Keep my focus on what stays
Body aging, still alive
Soul repaired by big brown eyes

Whenever I need focus
Lose anything I love
Brown eyes and blue skies
Call me back home.

I see brown eyes under blue skies
Enjoy sunny days, time to play
A life that's sweet, not pain free
Brown eyes fill my need.

Dollars

Meredith Cole

Happiness is success
Living more while having less
What will we get, what should we give?
Are dollars and smiles mutually exclusive?

Counting dollars makes us whole
Draining wallets to fill our souls
Wanting and wanting without a clear end
A miserable life with money to spend

Do businessmen wish they were artists?
Are they paid enough to be bored?
In the board room they sit
Asking what could have been
Finding no meaning in their means to an end

Does the engineer spend her years
Wanting a different life?
Like a prisoner in a cell with a window
Constantly looking outside

Money doesn't grow on trees
But we chop them down to make currency
What if we planted some instead?
The green on money can't compare to leaves

Do businessmen wish they were artists?
Are they paid enough to be bored?
In the board room they sit
Asking what could have been
Finding no meaning in their means to an end

What's the value of money when we're not here?
Do we still own possessions when we disappear?
Do we ascend to the heavens with deeds in our hands?
As our mourners fight over the rights to our land?

Do businessmen wish they were artists?
Or are they paid enough to be bored?
In the board room they sit
Asking what could have been
Finding no meaning in their means to an end

The Good Inside of You

Meredith Cole

I've listened to your embarrassing truths
And heard you tell some lies
But I think you want to be honest
About how you feel inside

You've shown mercy upon the weak
And trampled upon the small
But I know that within your heart
You can love them all

The bee dies when it stings
The dog can bark instead of bite
I see the good inside of you
I see you love and do what's right.

You see the worst within yourself
And call it "honesty"
I know that doing good is tough
Because it takes more energy

I have an X-ray of your heart
I see in you what you can't see
I love you both for who you are
And who you want to be

The bee dies when it stings
The dog can bark instead of bite
I see the good inside of you
I see you love and do what's right.

Launching

Allan Cole

It takes years to plan,
Needs wisdom and trust,
A middle-aged man
Two daughters so loved

Harder to protect them
Has he prepared them
For the losses and wins
To take care without him?

Curious and smart
It's time to take their shots
Dreams taking form
Learning who they are

Launching them today
He bows his head and prays
Ready or not
Love paves the way.

Event Horizon

Meredith Cole

Two lovers lost in space
Just you, me, and the stars
We floated around Venus
Spent a day or two on Mars

For a second I look back
Deciding to move onward
Soaring through the cosmos
I fly back instead forward

I hold on with all my strength
You still fade from my view
The event horizon pulling me away from you

The airlock sucks me in and spits me out
Soaring through the void, I can't slow down

A family of astronauts
As close as can be
We always stick together
Without the gravity

But sometimes orbits change
So unexpectedly
Making our way 'round the sun
Without the certainty

I hold on with all my strength
You still fade from my view
The event horizon pulling me away from you

I watch while heavenly bodies collide
While orbits change and Saturn's rings fly

Stuck behind the asteroid
That exists within my soul
Steering my rocket in circles
Like an extraterrestrial

I hold on with all my strength
You still fade from my view
The event horizon pulling me away from you

I want to see the stars I've never seen
I always find myself stuck in between

My Biggest Fan

Meredith Cole

Old automobiles
Casinos, stars, and cruise ships
Only wears high heals
But she's not afraid to trip

Always leaves the house
With a ribbon in her hair
A cheetah-print blouse
She looks so debonair

When I'm down
I make it through
You're my biggest fan
And I'm yours too

She tells me she loves me
I say "I love you more"
The most important VIP
Beautiful as she was before

Stories of the past
Love letters from the heart
Vivacious and steadfast
Timeless like a movie star

When you're down
You make it through
You're my biggest fan
And I'm yours too

Did you come into the world too early,
Or was it that I came too late?
Too many states between us
Months have passed since I've seen your face

When we're down
We make it through
You're my biggest fan
And I'm yours too

When we're down
We make it through
You're my biggest fan
And I'm yours too

Can You Smell the Honeysuckle?

Meredith Cole

Big carp swimming
I imagined catching one
Never had a fishing rod, though

Sunlight dimming
Below the leaf canopy
Listen to the summer breeze blow

Queen Anne's lace
The sound of pace
Do you smell the honeysuckle?
Years come and go, as the maple trees grow
Till I come back to my special place

Not a creature in sight
Where do animals hide?
Under lily-pad blankets and in tree-trunk lairs?

A family of ducks
And little chipmunks
The peaceful water and the crisp air

Queen Anne's lace
The sound of pace
Do you smell the honeysuckle?
Years come and go, as the maple trees grow
Till I come back to my special place

Walking together
In the beauty around us
Saying hello to the people that pass

Ripples in ponds
A chorus of birds
Heard from the trees to the bugs in the grass

Queen Anne's lace
The sound of pace
Do you smell the honeysuckle?
Years come and go, as the maple trees grow
Till I come back to my special place

Lazy Songwriting

Meredith Cole

ABAB seems so easy
Use less letters, eliminate terms
It's math, you plus me equals love
Which perfectly rhymes with "up above"

La la la
Na na na
Use syllables, don't think of words
People are so incredibly chiding
What's so bad about lazy songwriting?

I can compare
Love to addiction
A drug so strong, I'm on the floor
You've never heard that one before?

Whoa, whoa whoa
Yeah, yeah yeah-oh
Use syllables, don't think of words
People are so incredibly chiding
What's so bad about lazy songwriting?

Let's pick some chords, 1, 5, 6, 4
Sprinkling in similes and metaphors:

This song's as hot as the sun
Quiet as a mouse
Easy as pie
Big as a house

Oh oh oh
Hey hey,
Use syllables, don't think of words
People are so incredibly chiding
What's so bad about lazy songwriting?

Now is the time, where I drop some rhymes
Pure innovation, simply divine:

"Love" with "above"
"Heart" with "apart"
"Dance" with "chance"
"Baby" with "maybe"
I'm quite the lyricist, yes I am,
I do not like red beans and spam!

Shoobedoo
Doo ba da
Use syllables, don't think of words
People are so incredibly chiding
What's so bad about lazy songwriting?

Irish Hills

Allan Cole

A cold green sea wraps lush emerald spaces
Brisk salty winds blow on dry ruddy faces
Smooth ancient rocks feel white frothy waves
Among the faithful, some go, and some stay

Clouds get heavy, move at different speeds
Early morning mist floats from thick sappy trees
A few chirping birds dot a gray sky above
A few lonely people sing songs about love

A sacred Spirit hovers over cool earthy smells
Silence gets broken by rings of distant bells
On a weathered wooden bench on a moist mossy hill
Sits a man who remembers life when he wasn't ill

He's long wondered why faith so divides
Why small differences cause fractures so wide
Why the one who came so all may live and love
Is the one in whose name we cause so much strife

Ancestors came from these open hallowed shores
Searching for a life that could give them and theirs more
Sitting on that bench with the Spirit above
He gives thanks for people—near and far—who offer love

A sacred Spirit hovers over cool earthy smells
Silence gets broken by rings of distant bells

On a weathered wooden bench on a moist mossy hill
Sits a man who remembers a gifted life—and stories to tell

A sacred Spirit hovers over cool earthy smells
Silence gets broken by rings of distant bells
On a weathered wooden bench on a moist mossy hill
Sits a man who knows that with his soul it is surely well.

Singing in the Acid Rain

Meredith Cole

Everything we knew is gone
After they dropped the bomb
A place we once called beautiful
Sunrises have turned into nuclear dawns

How has humanity come to this?
Mutually assured destruction was no lie
We destroyed our Earth alone
Humans destroyed humankind

Wake up and smell the burning roses
Take a walk down dreary lane
Can you hear? The birds are screaming
I'm singing in the acid rain

There's nothing like a nuclear winter
Children sled in irradiated snow
Snowball fights with balls of plutonium
Months have passed since the sun last shone

Pavements have cracked, buildings have fallen
A car has been burned and turned on its side
To the left sits an old, forgotten garden
But it's empty because all the plants have died

Wake up and smell the burning roses
Take a walk down dreary lane
Can you hear? The birds are screaming
I'm singing in the acid rain

The bridges have burned and the houses have toppled
The leaves on the trees decided to leave
The school and the parks, now distant memories
The loss of our world we are now forced to grieve

Wake up and smell the burning roses
Take a walk down dreary lane
Can you hear? The birds are screaming
I'm singing in the acid rain

Wake up and smell the burning roses
Take a walk down dreary lane
Can you hear? The birds are screaming
I'm singing in the acid rain

Empty Rooms

Allan Cole

Laundry scattered on the floor
Beds almost made
When you were feeling scared
Glad I was there

We talked and fell asleep
Gliding into peace
Bodies getting rest
Worries hurting less

Leaving can be hard
Feeling so alone
No matter where you are
You can always come home

Watching you become
Who you're meant to be
Wanting to protect you
Make your life easy

There's so much to love
So much to do
You're just getting started
Make sure you stay you

Leaving can be hard
Feeling so alone
No matter where you are
You can always come home

Life is your teacher
Hard lessons come our way
Memories hold our love
New ones made each day

You held my heart
From the moment you breathed
Each day I have with you
Gives me what I need

Loving you is easy
Letting go, so strange
Wherever we go
We'll surely meet again

Leaving can be hard
Feeling so alone
No matter where you are
You can always come home

Leaving can be hard
Feeling so alone
No matter where you are
You can always come home